More Exhibitionism

Poetry and Prose from the York
Spoken Word open mic.

Edited by Glen Taylor

Stairwell Books

Published by Stairwell Books
70 Barbara Drive
Norwalk
CT 06851 USA

161 Lowther Street
York, YO31 7LZ

ISBN: 978-1-939269-49-2

Printed and bound in the UK by Russell Press
Layout design: Alan Gillott
Cover Photographs ©Alan Gillott
Edited by Glen Taylor

Publisher's note

The Exhibitionists was published in 2008. We had just arrived in York and finding no platform for poets started the monthly *The Spoken Word* open mic located at The Exhibition Hotel in Bootham. While in the USA we ran an open mic in Connecticut and astonished by the quality of the poetry we published an anthology to celebrate this collection of wonderful writers. In York, we were equally amazed and promptly published an anthology of our faithful regulars.

The Exhibitionists was the second book published by Stairwell Books: *More Exhibitionism* will be our fiftieth. We have many people to thank along the way not the least, Nick David, who insisted we published his novellas under our imprint and many others who have encouraged and supported us. In the event we also published an annual themed anthology on subjects as wide as the green man, trains, ghosts and the French (celebrating the Tour de France). This year, eleven years after founding *The Spoken Word* we are returning to a general anthology with submissions focused on those who have been associated over the years with the open mic.

These books are named after The Exhibition Hotel, and the staff and especially landlady Shuni, officially named Michelle Davies, who have welcomed us to their conservatory.

Over the years, we have been supported by a small army of interns and Glen Taylor, a student (now graduated) from York University, drew the short straw to develop and format this latest anthology. He has done a marvellous job earning accolades from many of our contributors for the sensitive and amazing letters of rejection and helpful comments with the accepted material.

We, of course, look forward to another 10 years and further fifty books and *Even More Exhibitionism* in 2026.

Alan Gillott & Rose Drew

Editor's introduction

I will admit, when I realised the sheer amount of words coming into my inbox, that I was a little bit daunted. Even as a student of English Literature, the enormous quantity of unfiltered text made me somewhat apprehensive. I'm used to reading things that someone in a position of influence has already deemed to be worthy of attention.

However, when I forced myself (with some gentle prodding by Alan and Rose) to open the emails and flick through the various submissions, I was truly blown away by the quality of writing and how much people had invested into their work. Every submission ended up capturing something that dragged me out of myself for a moment and though a lot of material could not make it to the final draft, I can honestly say that no rejection was easy.

As the choosing process went on I began to see time developing as a theme across the various pieces. Of course in any narrative that has progression there has to be some movement through time or either reflection of the past or projection of the future, but the pieces seemed to push a little further than that. There seemed to be a preoccupation with the nature of change; with moments of transition; with anomalies. There are grand sweeps through history, brushes upon memories and snaps of the future.

I hope you take the time to read and reread the poems and prose within this book and repay the time put in by the many writers who have submitted a piece of themselves.

Glen Taylor

Table of Contents

Morning Dew

6:40am to Anywhere
Hannah Stone

The world tilts, the streams drain down glass. Fat
rivelets race, buffet one another, secure of their legacy.
Spent commuters lean in and wish for...for...for?
Back gardens, fences, patios, conservatories,
dingy stations that retreat gradually from the eye.

The train screams and shudders, a whipped horse,
a victim. Stolen away in the night to a destination
as foreign as a glaciar, familiar as ice chinking glass.

Blue jackets circulate veins of veiled order, as I,
an odd fraud, pop and fizz words, among suits,
lattes and cappuccinos. Outside the jumble of life
blue green grey, mostly grey, shakes itself awake.
A black lamb in a field shivers off the dew. ⁄⁄

Lying in Bed on a Sunny Morning
John Gilham

A cat crosses the terrace beyond my windows.
She pauses to look in at my bed,
arranged so the morning sunshine
warms my body; aligned so these eyes
can take in the tiny, unimportant happenings
of leaf, insect and bird - my reduced world.

I am confined to a room, helpless, yet I bask like a cat
in the caress of light and air.

This is the same man, these are the same hands
that on brilliant mornings long ago
stroked you from sleep into loving.
This same sun, this same warmth, but a different languor
stretched us - along, around, inside each other -
hours together, feeding on lips and tongues and eyes
until we knew every hair, every freckle, every mole
anywhere under the sun.

Do you now, tending this sick body, think of those days?
or when we warmed your pregnant belly,
or when our children curled their little toes in bliss
naked as sunbeams? I wonder, but dare not ask.
I doubt you bargained for this final act of love
which I can never give you back or, love, repay. ⁄⁄

Old Father in the Café
Grant Tarbard

The old father speaks in a riddle of
crumpled time, just spare hankies
in his coat, out of tune with the season.

The old father speaks rapidly, yak-yak,
in a hitherto unknown flamingo language,
all gestures and ticks with a voice that smokes itself.

The old father's head is broad and flat,
like a piston stamping out a steel saucepan
with his boxed cranium of lobster shells.

Old father moves rigid, dust being remodelled
in the light of the air, like old books at the back
of a library found after a long absence.

Old father removes himself from the café chair,
bones play the creaking tune of arthritis, a hand cranked
music box weaving through the peaceable streets. ⁄⁄

The Fascination of the Mundane

David Younger

This small, grey world is not all bad,
the mould doesn't spread right through,
some bit of junk in that old shed
may fetch a line or two
if brushed by an observant eye,
a heart that doesn't seek to lie
but tells things as it finds them, as they are.

There's poetry in your spare room
and underneath that chair,
there's truth in every rusty spoon
and in the shoes you wear,
there's nothing more poetic than
graffiti on a Transit van
that rattles down suburban streets at dawn.

You don't need Troy or Tir na n'Og
or Wordsworth's daffodils,
you don't need legends bold and big
complete with twists and thrills,
a pile of dog shit by the curb
can conjure up the most superb
romantic verse, if only you will sing it. ⫽

Lost in the Wood

Hannah Stone

'Come-bye, Jack!' a call startles the silence.
My feet, negotiating latticed tree roots, falter;
flurrying thoughts pause.

On the ridge across the gully
a striding silhouette works his collie;
scurrying white shapes are stubborn sheep.

The path twists round; streams emerge
from their limestone cache and chatter to me;
the shepherd's left behind.

I envy his sheep.

Summoning a commanding voice, I project
the instruction to my wayward brain –
'Away! Away to me! Stand!'
Lie down.'

'I'm a little lamb that's lost in the wood...', line from Someone to
watch over me, Ira Gershwin, 1926. ⁄⁄

Moorhen
Val Horner

Gallinula chloropus - small water hen,
yet poorly made for swimming, no webbing
between your horny toes, so cannot paddle like
dabbling duck or glide like stately swan but strive,
these mad march days, to butt your way up stream
with jerk and thrust of your dusky head, more
often content to skulk and skive among
the reeds or today seem pleased to flap up
onto our easy bank and then – surprise –
what elegant pea-green, red-gartered legs!

On land, unlike slow waddling duck and goose
or galumphing bulky swan, you scuttle those
buttercup yellow, web-less, long toed feet
legging it here and there, white tail bobbing
slate-black feathers agleam and oh – how strange
your face with ruby eye, bright scarlet shield
and gold tipped beak, you are a streak of flame,
unable to rest – not fully at ease in air
on land or stream, lacking a comfort zone,
my little dark familiar, welcome home. ⁄⁄

A Moment to Remember

Sea Mither
Orkney
Adrienne Silcock

All winter long I've lain on the sea bed
I've listened to the crash of waves
and the silent cries of drowning men
and had no strength to help them.
I know about the thunderous clouds
whose long darkness drenches people's souls,
whose rain fills streams and lochs
with precious minerals for the feeding geese
and causes the marsh marigolds to glow.

And I know about the gatherings of cackling trows
whose mischief may be only meant as fun,
but drives the men away.
But the Vore Tullye's time is now
and can't your hear my fingers crackling
down at Warebeth beach?
How I spit and roar at Teran
while he stirs one last boiling broth
before at last he skulks away!

And did you spot my head rising up at Birsay –
beneath the retreat and foam of tide,
a rock beyond the brough –
or a seal lifting its face from its briny confines...
And did you see the shiver and spread
of my seaweed hair in the Causeway's swirling pools?
Hear my history. This fragile peace that we'll call summer
sublimates the surety of Teran's squalls. ⁄⁄

Charity

Rose Drew

Browsing wistful in Salvation Army,
seeking that which cannot be purchased,
she wanders to the curtains.
Kitchen's cold this winter;
lacey scraps that guard the door inadequate.

Oh my, she whispers, stroking familiarity
slouched over a metal hangar,
wide and colourful print of Rousseau-esque flowers,
human-sized in dimension and boldness,
set to dazzle against pale linen.

She sees two matching chairs, upholstered in
this exact pattern,
morning sun slanting playful across their cheeriness.
No memory remains
of where she bought them,
undoubtedly new,
to brighten a single-mum's living room.

Christine too, is there,
neighbour,
ancient daughter of Mississippi tenement farmers,
bowed by years of work, sun, deficiency.
Oh my, the older woman sighs, caressing chair,
I remember this, my favourite pattern at the factory,
how I loved to sew up curtains made of this same fabric.
The same one. Really takes me back.

Oh my, murmurs the younger woman,
20 years into the future,
Christine, chairs, house, country,
not gone, just mis-placed.
Nothing is ever truly lost,
she decides,
but hidden, somewhere safe,
re-findable within the unexpected. ✐

Going Back

Val Horner

The lane was narrower than remembered, trees meeting
overhead created a tunnel through which vehicles could
suddenly erupt forcing him to leap onto the almost non-
existent muddy verge. The way was also steeper than
expected; indeed he had no memory of this sensation of an
endless climb. He began to regret leaving his car at the inn on
the old Gloucester to Berkeley road. It was mid-August but
sunlight filtering through the trees seemed to have lost heart
and already the afternoon was fading. Yet he strode on with
an air of purpose he was far from feeling, barely keeping at
bay the gnawing belief that this was utter folly; he should not
have come. Leaving here had been a bitter struggle, staying
away, as year succeeded year increasingly easy, so why on
earth return now? Unless to exorcise the recurring dream of
somewhere, half-hidden, door ajar, sun shafting through
grimy windows, a smell of rotting apples, a miasma of
despair; dreams from which he awoke agitated, bewildered,
almost afraid. He shivered, turned up his collar against the
touch of a wind barely noticed before and there at last ran the
track, unmistakable, leading away from the road, dipping
down to a hollow with a half seen gate and a narrow path
through a wildly overgrown patch of garden. Even now he
hesitated, half inclined to retrace his footsteps to where he
could feel the sun. But whatever had led him this far insisted
and opening the gate he shouldered his way through clinging
brambles, burdock and briar, to the cottage almost lost
beneath a press of ivy and creeper. The familiar low oak door
hung loosely giving a glimpse of stone flagged floor, one look
enough, he scarcely knew what he had expected, feared,
wanted, but could hardly believe there was something for him
here. The few sticks of a broken life that stayed lay shrouded
in the dust of years; yellow cobwebs hung from crumbling
ceilings in rooms even rats and spiders had come to shun. He
paused, listening, searching the silence and as he turned,
thought for a moment that he sensed a movement among the
branches, no more than the flap of a wing, the fall of a leaf,
the smell of a rose, the pattering of a squall of rain that
wetting his upturned face spoke of redemption. ✐

13

Poem for Kayden Clarke

Becca Miles

The soft faced dog
does its duty without judgement
gently nudges flailing fists
offers up coat to stroke
until the fear desists. Here,
my hands still clench,
clawing, wishing they
could rip away the screen
in strips and see
what should have been –

"I'm going to be the way I should have been,"
he beams,
his voice is high and hopeful,
punching past the walls
of flesh and pixels,
to show me what it is
to be a desert gifted rain, and

here below
one slogan sticks with me:
"Better to be judged by twelve than carried by six,"
while he was both, and more. For

here are all of you.
You wail and shriek,
in a language I remember
but no longer speak
at the apocalypse
that was his brief release. I want
to press,
face to face,
mind to mind,
and shake you,
and scream

THEY'RE PRONOUNS,
NOT BULLETS,
YOU SELF-CENTRED FUCKS.

14

But that is not poetry.
That is no way to sneak past
the barbed wire
between us, and I know,

I know
I *know*
all this rage
is blurring my vision.

Add that lens to all the rest
stacked up
between us,
these facts still smash
through all the glass
and send shards
slicing into me:

He had a knife,
and they had a gun,
and they made a choice,
and now he is dead. ⟍

Terence

Harry Gallagher

When I was at school, perfecting
the fine art of disappearing;
blending into blackboards, coat pegs,
white lined tarmac and the bonding
to be had in inventing nicknames,
there you were. Ill fitting the backdrop;
a boy's clothes not disguising
a voice and a manner which left you
no hiding place.

Sashaying in a hothouse
for the dragons it bred;
deliberately provoking
each beating you took.
Refusing to fit in with the rest,
who knew by instinct where
the invisible line was –
we picked it up and towed it.

Years later, long escaped,
I heard about you from my mum:
That Terence – he drowned in a canal, you know.
Well he was always a queer sort.

My Clockwork Rabbit

John Gilham

I was thinking today
about my clockwork rabbit,
my not-work rabbit.

How he went away,
and I didn't miss him, his tinplate
eyes and ears forgotten

until, fifteen, at least, years later
I was planting a tree in the garden
and up he came.

Alas poor rabbit, I knew him well.
His cogs and spring now rusted,
his eyes not bright, his tail now still.

And yet I knew his place
was under the earth, his reburial
an act of kindness, not dismissal.

I'll not disturb him again.
For now he also tells the story of the place,
like the cats, the hamsters, the goldfish,
and below them, the Romans, the mastodons, tyrannosaurs,
trilobites. ⁄⁄

Surviving
David Younger

After the flood we buried our dead,
discovered new species, renounced old gods,
committed to memory names we couldn't speak
and gathered the driftwood for our camps.

After the drought we lay like dead fish
baked by the hot sun, not daring to move,
the breeze brushed our gills, still we flapped not once
till we swam in the belly of a bird.

After the fire we smeared our skins with ash
and walked among the embers in bare feet,
we poked and stirred the spent remains,
the harsh lessons, the histories, the mistakes. ⧄

Watching the Clock

Hope Springs
Clint Wastling

Lionel had managed to get out. His nondescript appearance allowed him to fade into the background of any occasion and this time it was to his benefit. He pushed through the angry mob and somehow managed to get home without being lynched. He looked at himself in the mirror. "Not bad for a man of fifty!" he said to himself.

His wife patted his paunch. "Exercise is what you need."

"Exercise! I haven't got time for that, so the team have been developing this." He held up the blue tablets in a clear glass bottle.

"What are they?" His wife took the bottle and shook the jar. She opened the lid and sniffed. "Lichen."

"Yes, in part. It's an anti-aging drug. It really does knock years off you."

"And it works?" Hope asked incredulously.

"Of course. Well, sort of."

"That sounds more like it, what's the catch?" Hope was sceptical. "Charlatans have been claiming to have made such a thing for years and you expect me to believe that your team of scientists has succeeded where the rest of the world has failed."

"It's true." He pulled out his phone, "here's your best friend, Mandy, that grey haired old soak of a boss! This is her now..." He passed over the photo.

Hope scrutinised it. "Gosh it's just like going back to the Eighties! She looks twenty-five at most."

"Precisely!" Lionel shook the bottle. "I had to get them away. The only pills left in the world. How about it? If there was a pill which gave you a second life, would you take it?" Lionel held up the bottle and counted four torpedo shaped pills.

He looked at the instructions again. *Take one tablet with a glass of water. Warning, do not exceed the stated dose. Avoid alcohol.*

"The best thing you could do is destroy them." Hope attempted to snatch the bottle. "If those people find out you've got them, there'll be another riot."

"Who's going to tell them?" Lionel retorted placing them deep in his trouser pocket.

"And then there's the implication. How do you know I'd want to have an extra life-time with you? Don't you think one is enough?"

"I don't want to hear this! I've made up my mind. If they work for Mandy, they'll work for me!" He walked out of the room before his wife thought of any other sensible points to raise. He went upstairs, sat on the bed and thought; then he looked at the middle-aged man in the mirror. That image decided him it was worth a go. He packed a suitcase. Hope waited in the hall as he came down. Her face was more perplexed than angry but it made her worry lines look permanent.

"Does having it all again mean so much to you?" Her tone was more conciliatory.

"I need to give it a go. I made such a mess of my youth that I'd like to try it again."

"Someone famous said *youth is wasted on the young.*"

"George Bernard Shaw and he kept going to his nineties. Somehow I've been middle-aged since twenty-five."

"Twenty-one more like but that's why I love you. Constant, dependable and reliable..."

"You might as well have added boring," Lionel said.

"I wanted to spare your feelings," Hope joked. She reached out and touched Lionel's cheek, he almost responded before changing his mind and picking up the case. He stepped outside, smiled and waved. "If you change your mind, you know where I'll be." He gently closed the door on 23, Lavender Crescent and took the thirty-three paces to the bus stop.

As the bus rattled through the flat East Riding countryside he could neither find beauty in the vista or relief from his sense of foreboding. The tablets had been well and truly tested but he still had nagging doubts about using them. He'd hoped Hope would share his adventure particularly when she saw the before and after photos of Mandy. In hours she'd changed from a sixty-year-old harridan to a lithe twenty-year-old and that was over a week ago! Now she lived life to the full and until this morning none of the team had seen her at work. Even Hope's texts had remained unanswered.

The news of her change spread like wildfire through the vast research establishment and within an hour everyone was finding excuses to pop in and ask the same question. By luncheon the local press knew and not long after satellite vans of twenty-four hour news channels were parked outside the plant along with an angry mob determined to get in and get their hands on the rejuvenation pill. That's when the MD came in and armed police arrived at the scene.

Lionel's hand tapped his pocket and he felt relief that his precious cargo was still there.

The headlines in *The Mail* said it all. "Riot at Plant. Armed police open fire on angry mob. Two injured, one missing." Lionel read the paper as the woman in front tutted and trilled "Oh! My..." she kept repeating.

Lionel sat back in his seat watching the outline of Beverley Minster rise from the landscape and dominate the rooftops. The town wound up to the Minster and it was here Lionel decided to get off and join the throng of tourists enjoying the architecture and history. He walked until he reached the little hotel overlooking the Highgate Porch of the Minster. He carefully put the bottle down on the bedside table and stood at the window. The perpendicular gothic of the doorway reminded him of how brief life was. "Six hundred years, fifteen generations. *If only*..." He realised he was talking to himself and that he was alone in a room with a double bed. He looked at the bottle, poured a glass of water, picked up a pill and swallowed.

For a long time there was nothing, then a whoosh of light-headedness, followed by pains, aches and curious sensations of tightening skin and muscles. Lionel must have lost consciousness.

Sunlight streamed in through the window as he awoke then stretched. He didn't feel right. He stood and walked a few paces. He smiled, then grinned when his trousers slipped around his ankles. His clothes were all too big for his lithe body. He looked in the mirror and saw a young man. He couldn't help smiling. He postured with his renewed muscles before he tightened his belt and skipped down the stairs. On Wednesday Market he found a fashionable menswear boutique and spent nearly a hundred pounds on clothes. He kept admiring himself in the mirror.

"Dispose of these for me please." He passed the bundle to the assistant.

He whistled as he walked back to the hotel and winked at a couple of young ladies who giggled and nudged each other. He felt on top of the world.

His room was open. He panicked and ran across the landing. Hope sat on the bed clutching the bottle. Tears ran down her cheeks.

"Oh! Lionel, what have you done?"

Lionel took the bottle and scrutinised the contents. "Don't worry, take one, we can start again maybe have kids, anything's possible!"

"Start again!" Hope smiled, "You never let me finish my sentence. The last twenty-three years have been... well let's put it like this. Some of us are young in body and others are young in mind. I know which I prefer and besides..." She stood and held out her mobile phone.

"Who's that old woman?" Lionel asked.

"Mandy. I went to see her."

"Oh! Dear." Was all Lionel could manage to say.

Hope's hand sprang out and grabbed the bottle of pills. "And whatever happens, you won't be needing these again!" Hope tipped the contents down the plug hole and turned on the water. "You'll just have to face reality like the rest of us Lionel Springs!" She didn't bother saying goodbye as she closed the door quietly but firmly behind her.

The End

Put your lips together

Mark Connors

Traffic wardens do it;
I've heard them
while they penalise the late.
Councils need the money
to keep libraries afloat.
What's a family man gone wrong
whose hour got away from him
compared to greater good?

Postal workers are the same;
they know the news they bring us
can go either way:
a letter from a lover,
a doctor or solicitor,
birthdays, Dear Johns, sympathies.
They pucker up their lips
and hope that we don't shoot them.

Window cleaners do it best;
the higher they get
the more tuneful they become.
They've seen lovers joined on Mondays,
watched marriages implode,
the lonely busying themselves
by doing nothing in particular.
They suffer the futility
of clean windows on the outside.

There's work you take to work
and bring back home again.
I whistle while I do it.
These days will come and go
and there are worse ways to exhale. ⁄⁄

WPC Carol Queers

Ross Moore

WPC Carol Queers
Stood in the road
For fifteen years.
At traffic duty
She was chronic
The one fine day
Went catatonic
So now she stands
In quiet stagnation
Like an Anthony
Gormley installation ⧄

Lesbian Loneliness

Sue Lister

Magnolia walls house the non-absorbent thrones.
Dry voices whisper round the walls like leaves that fall
unnoticed.

Uniformed bursts of energy swirl according to the clock
Bringing this, taking that.

Weathered skin, brittle bones, ghosts of the past
Gather on these barren shores.

My life, my love, has passed away, leaving me hung upon the
thorns
of grief in a waste of loneliness.

Unspoken. Living too long in the shadow of social shame
I dare not rock the boat and she is buried forever.

"My love" I cry in the dark hours and hold her in my heart.
By day I pass as an ordinary old woman. ⁄⁄

Edinburgh 2005
Hannah Stone

After Klinghoffer, a fresh culture shock:
taut cadences dim to freighted silence
as we emerge outside, dazed, take stock
of sirens, streetlights, puddles, late newsprint
and the night birds stalking down Princes' Street
bare-thighed, teetering in white stilettos.
Next morning, sodden bark chips soak our feet.
There are tentsful of luvvies and wannabes posing;
we're all being British, complaining but queuing
for coffee, and loos, and fully booked gigs,
book signings, freebies, potential viewings
of famous writers, prize-winners, big-wigs;
Jacqueline Wilson's two hundred watt smile
and armoured fingers, which look rather tired. ⫽

Penni
Matt L. T. Smith

Penni was bad.
She was a bad penny.
She spelled her name with an 'i,'
so you could tell her parents
didn't raise her right.
No one was surprised
when she had to raise her right hand
in court, and swear to tell the truth,
they knew she'd tell a lie,
she said 'No sir, it weren't me
who stole those sweets
why would I?
I've got the pennies,'
speaking tongue in cheek,
no wait
open your mouth
that's a fucking stolen sweet!

People would gab
about the village chav,
the haves criticising
the have nots
who have knots
tied in their stomach,
nature's gastric band,
not because they eat too much,
but because they know to expect
to not be able to eat enough,
and Penni had had enough
of not enough
so she took the sweets
as Davey stuffed himself,
whilst pointing at her.
No one could see his hand
in the cookie jar. ⁄⁄

Mrs Sorensen Said

Joe Williams

Mrs Sorensen said
Ruby's not here today
and asked if we'd seen her
since yesterday home time
or knew where she'd gone.
We talked about how
it is very important
to tell a teacher
if something is wrong.
We talked about how
keeping a secret
is sometimes the wrong thing to do.

Mrs Sorensen said
Ruby's not coming back
because she has died
and if we are sad
it is OK to cry.
We talked about why
we don't talk to strangers
or go anywhere
without telling our mum.
We talked about how
keeping a secret
is sometimes the wrong thing to do.

Mrs Sorensen said
a man was arrested
and if he did do it
he will be locked up
for a very long time.
We talked about how
people help the police
if they see something happen
and they are called witnesses.
We talked about how
keeping a secret
is sometimes the wrong thing to do.

So I put my hand up.

Mrs Sorensen said
I was very brave. ⁂

Unsound

Ben Jones

There's a hole in my wall which the wind whistles through
And the wallpaper's moldy and calamine blue
The carpet besmirched with a decade of grime
And the pattern is lost to a happier time
The journals and books where my memories stay
Have mixed and submerged in a fearful array
The curtains hang tattered in woeful neglect
Where the mildew and fungus and beetles collect

There's a hole in the floor where the mice have a nest
Where the walls creak and groan like a cancerous chest
And a puddle emerges from under the door
Like a serpent, it winds on the laminate floor
Underfoot, fragments of crockery crunch
Still stained with the leavings of long ago lunch
There's a rattle and scratching of verminous claws
The spoon never stirs so the pot never pours

There's a crack in the window that lets in the rain
Where it runs in a rivulet right down the pane
The mattress is rotten and rusted inside
Bacteria thrive and amoeba divide
The ceiling is sagging from waterlogged beams
And catches the sunlight with putrefied gleams
Like powder, the plaster is fast in retreat
With its choking secretions, the air is replete

There's a trace of a life that was never fulfilled
Like a drink only sipped and then carelessly spilled
There's hope of a future and trinkets amassed
But frittered away and consigned to the past
The wires are old but the bulbs are still new
And pictures of vigor are hanging askew
As if from existence, vitality blinked
A carcass remaining though life is extinct ⁄⁄

Fitted Wardrobes – Sliding Doors
John Fewings

Biscuit carpet, flecked so lightly
Beige walls apologise politely
Tasteful picture – autumn scene
Tidy, antiseptic-clean

Pin-pleat curtains, even-spaced
Stand attentive – straight-laced
Neatly turned, the chocolate covers
Not rumpled by children or pets or lovers

Plumped up pillows in position
Cushions "scattered" with precision
Library books in neatened stack
Bookmark-dated when due back

This is the perfect camera shot
This is the public face
A life of straightened order
With everything in place

But cast aside the sliding doors with easy, graceful glide
Discover there the clutter – the reality inside.

Dishevelled suit, disgruntled coats
A worn-out ancient jacket
A two-man tent, a dead umbrella
And a stringless tennis racket

A bustling crowd of shirts and tops
All clamouring for attention
Cacophony of threadbare socks
Protesting their dissension

A frisby and a rugby shirt
Still caked in orange mud
A crumpled heap of hankies
Smeared with snot and streaks of blood

Slacks and jeans and trousers in crumpled disarray

Tumultuous heap of tracksuits never see the light of day
Wellingtons all caked with mud that once I meant to clean
Amidst a footwear riot with boot-boys on the scene
They jostle and they bustle – they're ready to go lootin'
And if you try to stop them then they'll surely put the boot in

A waterfall of jigsaw pieces springing from the box
And flattened beyond usefulness, a tube of shuttlecocks.
A sleeping bag (unravelled) joins the wild affray
Six Christmas packs (unopened) of deodorising spray
A pile of childhood comics, all suited to a boy
A CD-cases pyramid and a dog-eared cuddly toy

The doorbell chimes – I hasten the wardrobe doors to close
Descend to greet my guests, adopting welcome pose

"So, how are you?" they greet me.
"I'm good," I say, "I'm fine."
They step across the WELCOME mat
But they never cross the line.
We maintain social nicety that carefully ignores
The lives that we keep hidden inside smiling, sliding doors. ⁄⁄

Appeal to A House Sparrow
for Farrah
Paul Sutherland

Sparrow, Sparrow - they've taken my granddaughter away from me

Quick Little Phillip - they've taken my granddaughter away

In the bare thicket of a hedgerow the rain's trickling down

You chirp away, on your own today, chirruping half the day

My Settled Spuggie – you gone quiet, and now is only rain

Trickling winkling down through the thickset of a hedgerow

Homely Cheeper – I've spent a lifetime or more to you listening

Sailor of the Eaves – if you big ears, tilt your head listen to my plea

If you A Lost Soul Catcher, you biggest wings, bring her safe to me

Bird of Far Arrival – they've taken my granddaughtor away from me. ⁄⁄

Five Minutes
Alan Gillott

Five minutes.
Three hundred seconds
And counting slowly from one,
Two, Three, approximating the pace
Of Arthur Sullivan's lovesick maidens –
'Twenty lovesick Maidens We ee'
Is one means of passing long periods of empty time
Even when somewhere around seventy
Sixty-ten in French
I lose ten precious miscounted seconds.

From watching the classroom clock
I learned my roman Numerals
Aye, Aye Aye, Aye Aye Aye
Aye Vee or four Ayes
With vee for five,
Then Six and Seven
The minute hand nudging one thirty six hundredth
Of the way around the face
Chunk, Chunk, Chunk
Eight as in Henry the Eighth
Then Aye Ex is nine
Eleven is Ex Aye
One hundred and twenty one
One hundred and twenty two
The date on the face teaches the rest
Em Cee Em – nineteen hundred
Ex Ex El – that's twenty from fifty is thirty
Well it was a famous Bacon's sometime home
Not that I knew who he was
Two hundred and fifty seven
Two hundred and fifty eight
A minute hand that nudges in milliseconds
Without that satisfactory chunk
Marked in Arabic numerals
Teaches nothing

Then it is time to fiddle and wiggle
Nib pens are boring
Though the nibs
Manufactured by Joseph Gillott and Sons
Are a one minute wonder
My fountain pen too precious
But the new fangled Biros
Last only half a page
And leak in any pocket
The cap, a splendid ear wax device,
The shank
Delivers a spit ball
Or conveniently soaked blotting paper
Excavated from the inkwell,
A very satisfactory distance
Definitely an escalation
Of the classroom wars
Two hundred and ninety nine
Three hundred
One, two, three... ⁄⁄

Captured Moments

Take a Picture

Christopher Nosnibor

It's a beautiful day. The sun is shining, the sky a perfect
azure and completely cloudless. It was too good a day to
waste, and so a small group of us decided to go out. A short
car ride, the windows down, music playing. Loud. None of us
is that big on the breezy summer chart hits that play on the
radio, or on the kind of stuff that fill the compilation albums
that proliferate in stores through the warmer months, so we
have our own favourites on. We're laughing and talking and
occasionally singing along. We haven't a care in the world. It
feels good.

We arrive at the coast and park up close to the beach. Being
mid-week and quite early in the season, it's relatively quiet.
We all bail out and soak in the sun, the sea, the fresh air.
There's a cliff path that runs along the bay. The views along
there are spectacular and I suggest we take a walk. The other
two aren't so enthused by this suggestion at first, but don't
take too much convincing. It'll only be a couple of miles at
most, we can turn round and return at any point. There's a
small part of me that's disappointed, somehow. Perhaps it's
because I so desperately want some time alone with her, just
the two of us. But I soon forget this selfish thought, and we
head on up the path by the stream that runs to the beach,
that ascends and then cuts up to the cliff top.

The breeze is more noticeable at this higher level, but it's
gentle and warm. The scenes are every bit as spectacular as I
had anticipated, as I had promised, and as I had recalled. I
had been here before, many years ago. I had been a child
then, and my parents had taken me and my brother one half
term or summer holiday. It had been a perfect summer's day
then, too.

But it was all about memory. I didn't have any pictures of
that day, and nor had my parents as far as I knew. They were
never all that big on holiday snaps. And really, neither was I.
But in recent years, I've grown aware of the fact that my
memory might not always be so good, or that I may simply
want to have something to remember days like this by. I took
out my little pocket camera and snapped my friends and the
views along the coastline.

I am happy here, in this moment, and I never want it to end. The other two skip on ahead while I make my records of the occasion. I'm aware that she has hung back and stayed with me. Right now, she's just behind me. I can feel her presence, and maybe even hear her breathing. Or maybe not: the breeze and the gentle scooshing of the waves against the rocks and washing up the sand on the beach in the cove below cover such tiny sounds. But I like to think I can hear her breathing gently at my shoulder.

She looks at me, smiling. The wind gently blows in her soft hair, the sun catching the movement and highlighting the subtle tones of her tresses. She leans against a rock and holds her arms, bare in her sleeveless cotton summer dress, out by her sides, spreading her fingers like a leaf unfurling or a butterfly spreading its wings to draw optimal warmth. She looks perfect: this is the way I want to remember her, always. I want to freeze-frame the here and now and to hold it for an eternity. But there's something... just something... indefinable. It's just beneath the surface. I can't see it and I can only vaguely sense it even now. Her eyes are shining... or are they grown slightly glazed? Is there something more behind them? Is that true joy? Or is it perhaps slightly forced? Is she hiding something behind those big brown eyes of hers? The smile looks natural, unguarded, joyous, unrestrained. But the longer I look at it, the more fixed and unnatural it appears to become. Is she feeling the same elation, the same sense of occasion, the same sense of perfectness that I'm feeling? I truly believed so.

They say a picture speaks a thousand words. But a picture never shows what's just out of the frame, what's going on behind the lens, or behind the eyes of those in front of it. And so the mind constructs its own narrative around the image. I'm sure it happened the way I remember and was the perfect day I recall. We ran to a high point on the cliff path and sang about the view. I – we – were in love with life, with the world, and things would stay that way forever: we promised one another that this was how life would be.

But life isn't like that. I can't even completely trust my own recollection now and wonder if I'm perhaps misremembering. It's not like I can very well go back and relive it other than in playback in my own mind. It's not like I can go back and ask her if she remembers it the same way I do, because it was the last time I saw her. She went away to university a week or so later. I wrote to her once, maybe twice, but she never replied. I don't even know if she received my letters. The whole crowd had dispersed and I moved away a few months later. Things were never the same again, and we all lost touch. I heard variously that she went missing or got married to some strange guy from overseas that she met at university, and left the country. Looking through the photographs now stirs a strange mix of emotions. I remember that day so well. But I don't think of it all that often. ⁄⁄

Soonest mended
for George
Mark Connors

You look like I've just stabbed your mum.
You're five and will get leeway,
but Jesus, boy, your unforgiving eyes.

It was you who cast the stone
I hit for 6 into Ullswater
but *that* look damn nearly felled me.

Your plastic spade is broken
like the fragile bond between us:
each shattered in *that* moment.

All my good work counts for nothing:
pizzas that I bought you with,
(your dad only gets you fun size),

light sabres whittled
from storm-strewn branches,
laugh-out-loud walking songs.

But there's a mountain pass I know
awash with thin grey slate:
a rookie skimmer's paradise.

Buttermere awaits us.
You won't forget *this* afternoon.
Get ready to forgive me. ⁄⁄

Eclipse

Hannah Stone

Sky opaque as Tupperware is standard
in Central London; eighty five percent
of sunlight blocked from southeast England
fails to cast apocalyptic gloom

on suited men, who beetle underground
en route to mining the nation's wealth,
while street sleepers slither from sleeping bags,
modern mendicants with Starbucks begging bowls.

It's not darkness, but the sudden chill
that drills into your consciousness
as mercury shows a three degree drop
and for a few moments exhaled breath spirals

in white bursts round buds breaking
on peeling plane trees. Tell it to the bees?
Maybe, but it's bones that register
the last ice age, sense the one to come. ⁄⁄

Gooseberries

Val Horner

Gooseberries yellow not green
split their hairy skins
and oozed stickiness
rough on the tongue
a taste like grimy sunshine.

A tortoiseshell butterfly
caught in the leaves feebly
beating a ragged wing
crumbled at a touch leaving
dust on greedy fingers.

In the shuttered room, I tugged
at my father's sleeve, but he
wept, incomprehensible tears
and would not be drawn away
into the fruit fall of my world.
Now kneeling in your garden
where gooseberries were always green
I stifle dry sobs with dirty hands,
not looking at the window,
where your smile slowly stiffens. ⁄⁄

Base Camp

John Gilham

There are those for whom getting to the foot of Everest
is harder than getting to the top for those who have.
And especially now, when Base Camp
is a dump of abandoned packaging,
where uneaten pizza rots, cylinders pile up;
and now is when the queue forms at 28,000 feet
to get to the summit. Mallory and Irvine,
Hillary and Tenzing, had it all to themselves.

It's time now, not to celebrate the winners
but time to remember those who in the end
pack out the shit, the waste, the empty Coke cans,
those who receive no glory, whose photos never make
the local rag – "ANYTOWN MAN ON TOP OF THE WORLD!"

Survival at the top, supplied with everything
a plundered world can velcro on is not so hard.
Not so hard as working sixteen hours a day
to stitch survival suits, to mind machines
that spill out insulated wrap for burgers,
non-degradable in mountain air.

It's time perhaps, we narrowed the gap
between those who think their junk-free place is at the top,
and those who scavenge on the shore,
who harrow the garbage dumps for what discard might
lift them a few feet out of the mire,
up from the bottom of the world. ∥

First Timer

Louise Mason

Sweaty palms
Pumping heart
Throat tight
Breath out.

Voice quavering
Papers in hand wavering.
Fumbling, mumbling an introduction,
Oh Lord, I'm still talking.
Now just waffling,
Did I even get the title right?

Clammy hands
Dry mouth
Pulse racing
Breath Out.

Look down, look down,
Concentrate on getting the words out.
Oops read that bit wrong,
Look up to see if anyone noticed?
Oh shit!
They're all looking at me.

Rabbit stuck in headlights
Mouth open
Eyes blinking
Mind blanks.

Look down, look down,
Force some more words out.
Remember something about eye contact!
Look up.

Panic ensues.

Picturing them naked.
Oh shit! Why did I do that?
Burying head in the book,
Just read the words on the page.

Shaking hands
Trembling voice
Deep breath

Dramatic pause

Not for effect, just randomly, never mind, the end is near.
Blurt the last word out.
Nod.
I'm done.
Scurry away to my chair at the back of the room. ⁄⁄

Last Visit to My Favourite Aunt
Grimsby Beach, Ontario, Canada
Paul Sutherland

I asked if I might stay. She, no longer
used to being a hostess, still consented.
I discovered she stored her flour bags
in the big Westinghouse oven. Perhaps
wore pink pyjamas bottoms on her head.
I had been told she was losing her mind
as if a delicate ball catapulted into space.

 Later, that same evening, she cooked
repeating I have nothing in but gathered
stray ingredients to create the substance
of a meat and vegetable dinner. For sure

she knew I was her middle-age nephew
who once dangled from the pine's tyre-swing
then a youth who protested the Highway
tearing down her husband's maple archway
which had protected her and the hamlet from

any harm. Soon, she would have to be confined
for her own good and neighbourhood peace.
She might after all walk down to the shore
and not recognise where pebbly land ceased
or flit about her breezy kingdom like a blue jay.

That night I slept in the same bedstead
as when a pimply kid or rebellious teen.
Now I noticed sky-blue walls, that the elm
shelving and headboard harmonised; each
revealed how she had cared for husband and
children, land and cottage, the community
with a sense of duty inseparable from love.

With morning, I waited for her descent.
Painstaking she tempered her way down
stairs and arrived with each item in kilter.
Serving breakfast, in a gust she asserted
frontier rights and wrongs, challenging
my failed marriage and rootless ways.

I asked forgiveness for a far off offence
when, a touchy adolescent, I wouldn't grasp
her already wrinkled hands and dance
at a wedding feast with my favourite aunt. ⁄⁄

Lost Time

Song of Lemminkäinen's mother

Adrienne Silcock

(i)
He's stepping out
all shine and feather.
Love and lust and loveliness
are bound to blot out reason.
What child listens to its mother
though they're knit in one mesh?
(ii)
I bade him not to go. He went.
I bade him listen. He did not.
I bade him, if he must, journey south.
He journeyed north.
There's no quenching a lad's thirst for danger.
Reason is a cloud that flits across the sky.
When the sky was clear, he breathed a sigh.
(iii)
I knew he'd head for Tuonela River*
its rage of fast-flowing currents
its spume claws and crunch of hungry molars,
though it'll be the velvet deep that defeats him
the apparent harbinger of peace
the lethal sweep beneath.
(iv)
Cruel sign, the bloodied hairbrush
– in haste, even vanity forgets –
he'd sworn he'd packed the lot
but there, upon his bed, lying careless
the grab at my throat
the war drum in my heart.
I, too, journeyed north.
(v)
Traces of his body at the water's edge
but not the whole –
Death's sons have intervened.
A mother's tears are made of glass,
splinter across the flow.
If only I can find the parts,
it must be possible to sew the cure. ⫽

* Tuonela river – the River of Death in Finnish mythology.

Distracted

Rose Drew

Bone strain leads
to bone adaptation leads to thoughts
of the last few months:

A potential child. No potential child.
And blood, devastating buckets of gore.
I can't focus. I can't read this article.
I run through old text messages,
one from him: *"you made*
me laugh!" sent October 20 when IT
was still Potential.

Train rocks and sways;
two girls giggle
and one stumbles onto me. *Sorry!*
she blushes. She looks to be five, maybe six,
her sister a young 20.
The disparity between my Teen and Potential
had intrigued. *Stop*
thinking of this I sternly insist.
Such thoughts.
equal useless pain
over an unfixable event
in the body of a woman nearing fifty.

Loading parameters. Peak bone mass.
Higher than customary strains
parallel
Vasectomy. Sterilization. No more of them! None!
This strikes too many soft spots,
revives foolish, expired hopes; distraction from Real Life.

Customary bone strain stimulus. In vivo.
Loading events. Peak strains: March 2010, June 2011,
and now somewhere between late October,
when ultrasound displays a lifeless form,
to November 8 when the rest of It departs,
following its potential.

Reduction of strain, increased loading,
decreased family, increased distraction,
higher than customary strain stimulus:
in vivo loss. ⚄

Delete

Tom Dixon

In a grey room, the walls made from breezeblock framing a bare concrete floor, Andreas watches his screen with eyes full of childlike wonder. He watches tapes spool, tapes rewind and tapes playback. It's one of his favourite things to watch that remain in the public domain.

The pipeline brings Andreas another capsule, his third of the day. The pipe whooshes and spits the new capsule into the cradle on his desk. He unscrews it and reads the new instruction.

He presses save though he has made no edits and drags the file across the screen to the folder marked 'work'.

The new instruction will be simple. Delete, date, time and channel. They rarely deviate.

During orientation, the video made it clear how deletion was the only way. Head office had tried editing; even pixilation but there was no way of placating the braying masses. They cried, they wailed, some even gnashed teeth and without fail, they all got their way in the end.

They cut, hacked and spliced until the past made no sense but at least no one was upset anymore. They were just confused. Which was fine, the confused could be medicated, directed and generally led. You can't complain if the word 'complain' is merely a jumble of meaningless letters.

Andreas types in a series of letters and numbers, and hits enter. A file appears on his screen. He opens it and watches as the opening credits of a game show from a time before he was born appear on his monitor.

He will be the last person to view it.

Andreas doesn't have to watch it. The footage has been marked for deletion so all he has to do is press delete.

But he does watch. He searches the faces on screen. The smiling faces of the dead, mugging to the camera and attempting to squeeze in their catchphrase that no one remembers anymore. He wonders what they did to end up marked for deletion. Which one of them spoiled it for everyone else.

He can't watch for long. Even he's monitored nowadays.

Three minutes pass and then he hits delete.

The pipeline remains silent so he double clicks on the folder marked 'work' and watches the tapes spool, tapes rewind and tapes playback with eyes full of childlike wonder. In his grey breezeblock room, the ceiling a tangle of silent, for now, pipes, Andreas waits. ⫽

Your Revolution
Joe Williams

Whatever happened to your revolution?
You're working for Barclays, you're up for promotion
Back in the eighties you'd rage against Thatcher
This time next month you'll be regional manager
Congratulations, you've made it in banking
You're queen of the high street, your CV's outstanding
How does it feel to be part of the team
In the faceless, exploitative, corporate machine?
Whatever happened to rights for the workers?
You fought against poll tax, you marched with the miners
But look at you now, is this what you are?
With your personal pension, your company car
Where did it come from, this ruthless ambition
To rise through the ranks to a higher position?
Whatever happened to your big ideas?
Wasted on fixed term investments and mortgage arrears ⁄⁄

Butcher's Row

Mark Connors

You can still buy a pig's head here for two quid;
someone should tell the prime minister.
The smell never bothered me as a kid
But, these days, that cloy of dead meat,
the same zing on the tongue when you lick batteries,
notes of copper coins and long-rusted bikes
from rivulets of blood that trickle down these indoor streets
when apprentices mop out the shops,
has me near hurling up the cous cous from my lunch.
My dad would be appalled I'm meat and dairy free
if the aforementioned hadn't helped kill him.
And yet, I walk these bloody gauntlets
(the smell far worse than the market's reeking gents)
now and then, just to reminisce; a bus trip
to Leeds to time it perfectly for price cuts:
a bleeding bag of spare ribs, Irish style,
free of fancy marinades, just a rapid boil
till the water turns to a lardy milk,
a beat before the flesh slips off.
Then over to the tripe stall for a haul
of off-white slime no animal should eat.
I think it's the same woman 30-odd years on;
it doesn't seem to have done her much harm
other than taking all her teeth but one.
Dad never bothered with the onions –
he wouldn't even cook it. We ate it
fucking raw! It was child abuse via cow's stomach lining.
Yet, with a bit of salt and a lot of vinegar
it went down a treat on those Saturday nights
while we watched *The Generation Game*. I leave
the way I came, the same knot in my gut
I walked in with. I head for Holland & Barratt's
for pretend meat that won't linger in my bowel. ⁄⁄

Midnight

Eulogy
Jennie Owen

Riding your shoulders
so high I touch the leaves,
squinting at the sun.

Dungeness fish hut.
Briny prawns, warm in newspaper.
Pebbles and hot blue.

You name all the birds,
as we pause and cup our ears
the nightingale sings.

Searching for glow worms,
dawn streaks the sky pink and grey.
The woodland shivers.

A swirl of starlings:
inky water in the dusk,
deafening the stars.

Your name preserved in
the book covers, silver fish
and musty foxing.

Twelve jars of honey
numbered in black marker pen,
we took from the shelf.

Ghosting in soft dust,
binoculars pine for you.
The house leans away. //

Knowledge
Alan Gillott

I used to traverse the ancient woodland
Remarking all around flowers and leaves
In unusual juxtaposition
Spoor led to hidden dens
And the sound of birdsong
Soars with satisfaction
The gentle soughing steadies
My travels through myriad
Secret pathways

Now dense packed forest
Obscures the flowers
And the paths, should I find them,
Lead only to a specific destination
The songs warn of thrusting through the brush
For paths that are not there.
The creatures here are watching me
Marking every step
Observing every leaf I touch
Every fruit I taste
Because in this forest
I am the prey. ⧄

Out of the Woven Belly Button

Grant Tarbard

A clothed womb is my drunken cell, hangman
of this damned fool flesh, blood souring a yard
of my terrine's plush plum comfort in my
haberdashery years, trying patience.
I throw my arms wide and embrace my woes
in a ringlet of deceitful bullish
sloth. I am a burlesque bloated body,
a charity shop rat catcher hoarding
tiny skeletons and a shadow of
cadavers, spread eagled, wooden white eyed.
I am a pernickety old crow with
paper talons, flush of cheek. In woven
barley my own personal haunting played,
a phantom rattling the cage of the world. ⁄⁄

Hometown Homos

David Younger

A dust-coloured day in a soulless town,
the sky's thick wool, rain-damp and dark.
Some local lads are hanging round
the public toilets in the park.
They snap and snipe their spittled slights,
mouths of bile, all bark, no bite.
The filthy, piss-stained loos are scrawled
with crude graffiti cocks and balls
and unromantic invitations
to sodomitic fornications —
lads up for a fuck, not a fight.

I go for a piss in this sodden sty,
they heckle me as I walk out,
I try my best to dodge their eyes
as they begin to jeer and shout.
I wonder why they gather here
to ridicule a passing queer,
their pointless slurs too dull to prick
my pride, their smears that fail to stick
and yet build up, over the years? ⚋

The Deadly Morris Dance

Pauline Kirk

There can't be many company bonding days that end in murder.

The weekend started well. It was a lovely morning as Tony and I arrived at the Harrogate office. Jenny and Sarah were waiting. Dan from Design turned up soon afterwards. With me from IT and Tony from Human Resources, the management team was almost complete. Only Mick from Sales was missing.

Jenny's mouth was set in its usual sour line. "You're late," she called. I bit my tongue and smiled. We were probably being assessed already. Bill pretended to be an easy-going employer, but he was ruthless. If anyone failed to meet his standards, they were out.

Mick arrived in a Mercedes, driven by a stunning brunette. "This is Karen," he announced. "She'll be joining us for dinner." He made a big show of kissing her goodbye, no doubt for our benefit, before she sped off.

"What's this one called?" Bill demanded. We were used to Mick turning up with his latest date. At the barbeque it was Carol. Irena came to the Christmas meal. We didn't put a name on invitations any more, just 'Mick Plus One.'

"Karen Fosdyke," Mick announced proudly. Not that her name meant anything to us.

For a moment Bill looked surprised, then annoyed, but his smile returned. "Well, good for you," he replied amiably, "she's beautiful. Now let's find our hidden talents."

Everyone nodded vehemently.

The first two sessions went well. After orienteering up the Chevin, we went shooting near Otley. Then we adjourned to Darnley Court for lunch. After eating in the cafe, we trooped across the lobby to the private dining hall. "We're going to learn to Morris Dance," Bill announced.

"I didn't know we'd be *dancing*." Jenny sounded shocked.

"It's an excellent way of building team spirit," Bill enthused. "Everyone has to play their part, or the dance doesn't work. I've hired an expert to teach us an old English dance. Here he is!"

A newcomer entered the hall. He must have been sixty but looked fitter than all of us. "Afternoon," he said. "My name's Gideon and I'm here to teach you the Donkey Dance. Now, who's volunteering to be the donkey? I've got a genuine nineteenth century head for you to wear." He didn't sound like the country bumpkin we'd expected, more like a retired teacher.

Everyone looked around, embarrassed. The dining hall was grand but it was also long and cold. Glass doors faced onto an inner courtyard. None of the ancient windows fitted properly, and with an open door at each end of the hall, there was a fierce draught. I could see a similar room the other side of the courtyard, also with French windows. It looked like a library.

The tables and chairs had been pushed to one side, leaving space for us to practice. I hoped the room would be warmer with the velvet curtains drawn and reaching to the floor. Otherwise it would be a chilly dinner. "Come on," Gideon insisted. "It's quite simple. Six of you dance a jig around the donkey. At the end, the donkey runs down the middle and bounces off a trampoline. Here's one I made earlier, as they say." He pulled a small trampoline from the corner. "After dinner tonight, we'll put on a show for your partners and colleagues. They've already been invited, so you'll have to learn how to do it, won't you?"

"Blackmail!" Dan pointed out. We all laughed, but no one stepped forward.

"All right. I'll wear the Donkey head," Bill said. "Then at least we'll get started." It was a big, heavy thing. When it was on, his face was completely hidden. He looked like Bottom in 'Midsummer's Night Dream', but we didn't dare laugh.

All afternoon we learnt the dance, getting hot and tired. At first the jig was more like a scrum, but by the fifth attempt we'd got the idea. Bill was surprisingly fit, despite his ample midriff. Though he puffed and landed heavily, he became quite good at running up the hall and jumping off the trampoline with a flourish. There was a lot of shared laughter and banter. Even Jenny joined in. We were indeed bonding.

"Now for your gear," Gideon said, fetching a large basket. He took out a supply of white shirts, black trousers and black shoes, each carefully named. "Bill's PA guessed your sizes. You can swap if necessary. They're all the same. Here are the

66

bells to put around your right leg and left arm." He passed a set to Bill. "And here's your donkey costume," he added, giving him a patchwork tunic to pull over the shirt and trousers.

"Push me in the right direction, Tilly," Tony begged me. "I'm hopeless at this sort of thing."

At seven o'clock the 'other halves' and friends joined us. After an excellent meal, everyone waited expectantly. The waitresses stood in front of the doors to prevent interruptions. With the curtains pulled across the French doors and candles on the tables, the room looked quite cosy.

As the dance was short, we'd decided to do it three times. Between each Donkey bounce, Gideon would perform a jig of his own. At first all went as planned. We did the jig; the Donkey ran down the middle, launched onto the trampoline, *boing*, then landed on both feet. I noticed something odd soon afterwards. The candles on a table near the French doors blew out and a waitress had to light them again. I thought little of it. Gideon was doing an amazing sword dance. Everyone was watching and clapping when Tony whispered, "One of us is *missing*." Urgently we looked round. It was Dan. We were about to take our positions for the second Donkey Dance and Dan had disappeared. Sarah swore. All we could do was rope Gideon in to take his place.

Luckily the dance went well again. The Donkey skipped down the middle, jumped onto the trampoline, *twang*, then landed lightly on one foot. Gideon did an even more complicated solo jig.

By the third Donkey dance, we had six dancers again. Dan was full of apologies. He hadn't realized how short Gideon's sword dance was and had popped out for a smoke. "Idiot!" Jenny hissed. For once I agreed with her.

We did the final dance with Gideon watching from the side. The Donkey ran down the middle to the trampoline, launched himself with a *boing*, and landed to tremendous applause. He was the boss after all. Even our guests felt obliged to congratulate him.

They were still applauding when we heard the most appalling scream from the other side of the courtyard. I shall

67

never forget it. One of the waitresses had found Karen Fosdyke's body in the library.

It was chaos after that. Everyone ran to the exits to see what had happened. Jenny and I headed for the far door knowing it led to the lobby, but we were turned back by a waitress. I tripped over the trampoline, almost falling flat on my face. As I got up I noticed there was mud on the canvas.

After that, the police arrived. We didn't know Karen. Mick had only been dating her a few weeks. But it was awful to think of her being murdered. Sarah and Jenny started crying and I couldn't stop shivering. The poor woman had been stabbed with one of the steak knives from dinner. The knife was still in her back.

Our guests were sent home, with names and addresses noted, but we were detained. We weren't even allowed to talk to each other. That was when we realized we were suspects.

For hours we sat in miserable silence as each of us was called into the manager's office and questioned. My mind kept going round and round. It was the proverbial bad dream. How could one of us have killed Mick's girlfriend? We had all been dancing. It must have been an outsider. Yet the staff insisted no one could have entered the building. The outer doors were locked and there was a receptionist in the foyer. Everyone else was watching us.

I've always liked solving puzzles. I suppose that's why I work in IT. To keep calm, I started to go over what had happened. Karen's body was found in the library, which ran parallel to the hall. You could get to it by leaving the hall through the North door and going through the lobby. No one could have gone that way after the dancing started, without being spotted. There was another route however: through the glass doors, across the courtyard and into the French windows opposite. Our windows were hidden behind curtains, so perhaps someone could have sneaked out. But no one could have done that without disturbing our dance. Except Dan. In horror, I realized that Dan must be prime suspect. He was the only one who'd left while we were performing. No wonder he'd been with the police so long. I couldn't believe Dan would kill anyone, much less Karen. He'd only met her today. Besides, he hadn't been gone that long.

Then I recalled the candles blowing out. Maybe the French doors had been opened? The courtyard was paved but not particularly well: it was muddy in parts. And there was mud on the trampoline.

I couldn't help it. I looked up sharply towards Bill. He was sitting in the far corner, well away from us. Our eyes made contact and I felt a chill pass through me. Quickly I lowered my eyes. I couldn't be right. Bill was dancing the whole time. Besides, what motive would he have? He didn't know Karen was coming. None of us did until Mick introduced her. So if someone wanted to kill her, it couldn't have been planned in advance.

My mind was racing. The Donkey Dance would have been the perfect cover. Bill could have slipped behind the curtain to the French windows while Gideon did his sword dance. There were differences in the three dances. The first and third time, the Donkey sounded heavy. The second time, he seemed lighter and made more of it: he skipped. The enormity of what I was thinking made me feel sick. Dan was much lighter than Bill. What if Bill swapped with him? That would have given Bill time to sneak out. Maybe Bill said it was a joke, or that he was tired. Dan would do whatever the Boss asked. No one would have noticed with the tunic hiding the Donkey's body.

My theory was growing. The mud on the trampoline could only have got there if the Donkey had gone outside. Bill must have asked Karen to meet him in the library, and crept up behind her. Then he returned to do the third dance. "But why should Bill kill *Karen*?" The question pulled me up short.

He was surprised when he first saw her. Maybe they'd met before. Then I remembered the time Bill had gone to Mauritius to be married, but returned single. He'd never mentioned it, but office gossip said he'd been stood up at the altar. And his fiancée's name was Karen. Could it be the same woman?

How do you accuse your boss of murder? Dan would never do so but he must by now be realizing he had been used. If I accused Bill, I could kiss my job goodbye. And I had no real evidence. Yet I had to help Dan.

Feeling weak, I got up and walked towards the policewoman. ⁂

Ventriloquist
for Kane Holborn
Matt L. T. Smith

When he asked me to be his dummy,
I said to him
'You could at least buy me dinner first
before sticking your hand up my ass.'

A voice swells inside him,
his brain sends a message his tongue can't fold
into the right envelope.
Now it's my job to deliver.

The ventriloquist is a master puppeteer,
turned marionette,
unable to hold his own strings
he plays my vocal chords.
The words flying from my gob
hit tripwire
ricochet,
words detonate, prematurely,
dismembered limbs fall
from my mouth.
Don't shoot the dummy!
Messengers make mistakes!
But I wish a shot would ring out,
hit me like Teddy Roosevelt
and this dummy would carry on
lip syncing his diction
despite the bullet
to spite the bullet
I'd bite the bullet
to fix my screw-up.

Lodged, I can feel the lead
scraping. The Doctor peers in.
I feel his eyes down my throat.
He can't see anything,
no obstruction, whilst I'm suffocating,
choking on his cornea.
Every night I open wide

and a roomful of eyeballs
stares at the absence of tonsils
eager to take their place.

Retch, vomit, I can't
take to the stage,
leaving the ventriloquist voiceless for a day,
he thinks out loud,
telepathy keeps the crowd entertained.
He doesn't need a dummy,
just open ears to borrow.

I stare blankly,
jaw dropped,
no surprise, just empty.
No one there to move my lips.
Don't compliment a dummy.
It looks like the words come from my mouth,
it's not my voice
that comes out. ⧸⧸

It

Ben Jones

It crawled in through my ego
And prickled down my back
Muffling my senses in a symphony of black

It spoke in stolen echoes
Of a long abandoned place
Engraving Its design in every line upon my face

It sought to gain a purchase
With reason, Its disguise
A caution to be on my guard and not to trust my eyes

It locked the door behind it
Then melted down the key
And when It sat in full command, It changed Its name to Me ⁄⁄

I haunt

Jennie Owen

It isn't twelve bells pitch, lunar fat,
when phantoms roam.
They sliver in, creep and shiver in
pale spaces before dawn,
whilst grey day peeks,
on an empty horizon.

The Big Wide mutes, yawns silent.
Drags, lazy limbed and stretches. I,
a feverish eyed toddler, wraith to the last
thready streetlights,
peel back the skin.

Your warmth rolls away
Inch   by   inch.

It is hard to bear, this solitary duty.
To watch your eyelids, silt closed,
moon drunk sway. To know
behind them is midday sun.
My shadow exorcised.

Then I, always turning room corners,
follow small shallow footsteps
that flee. A heart flutter, just

out of reach. ⁄⁄

Glimpses of Tomorrow

"The spotted hawk swoops by and accuses me..."

Walt Whitman

Adrienne Silcock

It pecks at the air,
as if it were pecking at guilt
fluffing the fur of the kill
spilling it into the wind.

And then after that,
the first drop of blood
bright red and shining.

Afterwards, the flow,
and scrambled ugliness
which I don't want to think about
when all I can see now is beauty.

Which makes me wonder,
if there's a day when
suddenly beauty
drops below the horizon
following the sun,
but never reappears –
not even
a frail glistening of light
only a darkness,
a small murmur of breath
that burrows rapidly for the past.

It's like a mote of childhood
swept up and away
by adult wings. ⁄⁄

Squabs

Grant Tarbard

I will be the last out of the box
of the toiling bell's Trojan horse bow.

I will be the last orchid
to wither in your funeral wreath.

I will be the last rain drop
of the closing curtain of the coral sky.

I will gather in the shadow
of your crowing footstep.

I will be the flower of May,
whatever pebble that God scatters me on.

I will be the bawdy song crushed like a walnut
in the strongman's elbow.

I will taste the dove encased in a weep
in a harvest of virginal squabs.

I will be there, having a crisis of faith
that my hair wasn't really here at all.

I will be this for a thousand years,
my heart is never pure, my back is crooked.

I will feel the choke of the noose around my neck
and sing of independence with my last scratched breath. ⁄⁄

Born Again
Jacqueline Zacharias

Vivekaa shook the duvet and folded it on the edge of the bed before proceeding to dust the dressing table.

"Vivekaa! Vivekaa! Another cup of coffee for your appa! Hurry up, will you!" The call was shrill and commanding.

Sighing, Vivekaa continued to dust. These days, she was feeling slightly under the weather. Her eyes fell on her arms. They were pale, almost bloodless. In a month, she would be fifty. Fifty and alone. Fifty and still living in a prison called home, the wardens: her elderly parents who ensure the inmates do not break free. She placed her hands delicately upon her tiny breasts – denied of warmth and the caress of a man and the embrace of a child. Her own child.

"You and your sister will only be matched with men from our caste. No hybrids and aliens allowed," her father used to exclaim when she and her sister, Mina, were in their twenties. These soon gave way to their thirties and, by this time, their youngest brother, Ajay, had left home to marry his sweetheart, Haseena, a dark-eyed beauty who bore him an equally beautiful daughter.

"We have sent your uncle to the village back home to source suitable husbands for the two of you. He will be back with good news," their mother once quipped, before continuing to gorge on the crispy, spicy, potato samosas that Mina had fried for tea.

The sisters waited in anticipation but their uncle never came back. Instead, he had found himself a nubile, village virgin and decided to abandon his family back in England to settle for a new life with his pubescent bride.

Their thirties gave way to their forties. Their parents were now in their late sixties, less energetic, less eager in their search for spouses. Besides, it was clear that Vivekaa and Mina were useful to have around in their old age. Vivekaa was adept at cleaning the home whilst Mins was skilled in strict caste-centred vegetarian cooking. They both worked outside the home as well, earning a sizeable income between them, which was promptly handed over to amma every month without fail.

"I'm saving up for your future," amma used to explain but twice a year, she and appa would make trips back to their homeland, buying lots of presents for relatives and family friends. The sisters had never met any of them. Mina also suspected that her parents were generous in handing out cash gifts during these visits. However, the sisters never raised the issue, for they were never trained to be other than slavishly obedient to their parents. After all, parents were second in line to the Divine Creator, were they not? Filial piety at the expense of individual needs reigned supreme throughout their lives.

In a few weeks, she, Vivekaa, would be fifty. Fifty. This was her future.

"Vivekaa?"

Vivekaa awoke from her pondering. "Yes, Mina?" She placed the duster by the dressing-table.

"I've already made coffee for appa."

Vivekaa smiled tiredly. "Thanks."

Mina leaned against the wall, biting her lips.

Vivekaa whispered sadly, "You have another four years to go before you turn fifty." She looked out the window. There was still some overnight frost clinging stubbornly onto the branches of the trees.

"Vivekaa?" Mina paced listlessly about, unable to meet her sister's eyes.

"What is it? Is everything all right?"

"Hmmm..." Mina cleared her throat. "Vivekaa?"

"Yes?"

"I'm pregnant."

There was a hush. The twittering of birds echoed through their ears.

Vivekaa closed her eyes, holding her breath. Seconds ticked by.

"Vivekaa?" Mina bit her nails. Her hands were perspiring. Her heart pounded against her chest but the pulse in her belly beat steadily.

The silence seemed eternal as Vivekaa swam through a tunnel of dark warmth. Her limbs loosened as she slipped into a space of peace.

Tears welled in Mina's eyes as she turned to leave. Was her big sister mad at her for stepping out of line? Her big sister was her only ally in this world.

"Mina?"

Mina stopped. "Yes, sis?" Her heart raced.

"How many months...?"

Mina licked the tears off her trembling lips. "I'm into my fourth month..."

"And soon it will show..." Vivekaa spoke quietly. "Mina?"

"Yes, sis?" Nervously, Mina bit her nails. Terror washed over her face.

"The touch of a man... how did it feel?"

"Oh Vivekaa!" Mina burst out as she rushed to her elder sister. "It felt beautiful."

Joyfully, the two sisters embraced.

***

A Month Later

Stunned, Mina fell backwards as appa's fists smashed furiously onto her delicate cheeks. Instinctively, she clutched her belly, stumbling frantically to escape the next blow. Amma was in the kitchen, wailing and beating her long, heavy breasts.

What was she wailing for? Vivekaa wondered angrily. The expense of feeding another mouth? That she now had to budget her trips to her bloody homeland? An unexpected surge of hot energy coursed through her throbbing veins. It felt foreign to her nature, yet exciting. An incredible force propelled her forwards as she lunged to shield her little sister from further violence. She stood between appa and Mina, arms akimbo, her light skin red and inflamed, swimming with rage.

A tussle ensued. Appa pulled Vivekaa's hair and spat on her face. Undeterred, Vivekaa pushed her father against the wall, roaring, "Run, Mina! Run! Get out! Call the police!"

Mina was paralysed on the ground. "I will not leave you!" she sobbed fearfully, her fingers still gripping protectively against her small baby bump.

"Go!" bellowed Vivekaa, as she pinned her struggling father to the wall. Years of suppression and containment were now loose and frenzied like that of a wild, wounded beast.

Amma entered the scene snarling menacingly before hurling a kettle of boiling water onto Vivekaa.

Horrified, Mina screamed, scrambling to her wobbly knees as she dashed out of the flat.

***

"She's opening her eyes..."

"Did she say something...? I thought I heard a whisper..."

"She's highly sedated. You will have to wait another day or two."

Voices faded into the distance as Vivekaa sank into a deep, dark sleep. It was painless and peaceful.

***

"Here, aunty, drink this water."

Vivekaa managed a nod as she received the glass of water from her neice, Malika. Malika was eleven with a sweet smile. She felt the bandages around her aching face and neck. "Mina?" She turned weakly to her brother. "How is... Mina?"

Ajay patted his sister's hand, responding in a soothing tone, "Shhh... she's fine..."

"The baby..."

He smiled. "He's safe and well. Mina has been ordered to have complete bed rest."

"You must rest also, Vivekaa. We will come back tomorrow," Haseena added.

"And appa and..."

Cautiously, Ajay replied, "They have been arrested and charged... I will tell you everything when you are better. You

82

must stay with us for a while. We will look after you and Mina."

Vivekaa breathed deeply. In a few days, she would be fifty. Fifty and... and... she was at a loss for words. Closing her eyes, Vivekaa laid back on the pillow.

An untrodden path stretched before her.

Open and Free.

Fifty and Born Again. ⁄⁄

Terminal 1
Sue Lister

Misery incarnate
With indefinite leave to remain....?
No thanks – enough's enough.
I'm out of here
On the first available safe, easy, comfortable ticket I can find,
One way, no stops, destination confirmed.

Not for me the £10,000 gamble
Of a trip abroad: what if
The body warps, the mind flips, the money melts
And I'm left stranded?
Bloody British law needs changing
And that's a fact.

Wish I was a dog
Or any kind of much-loved pet.
Their suffering's soon ended,
Not like mine.
Just take me to the vet!

"God give me strength"
May work for some
But what about us atheists?
My life, my death, my choice!
That's all I ask.

I could do with a bit of peace and quiet
After a life lived with gusto and
Fully appreciated.
So, with many thanks to existence,
Thanks for having me...
Over and out
Sue. //

Free-Wheeling

Muriel Masson

I am a wheeler
I haven't always been.
For a third of my life now
My wheels have brought me
Freedom and a life
I'd thought lost forever.
There are the four wheels most people have
The ones that all equate to freedom
Or at least a comfortable way
Of easily and speedily
Going from A to B.
These, on their own, would do nothing for me.
But together with a little blue card
Some help with running costs and
My trusted oh-so-noisy stick
They conquer my beloved hills
And deposit me, rested,
Anywhere I need to be.
Most importantly, they also carry
What (to the eyes of the world)
Really makes me
A wheeler.
THAT's where freedom TRULY begins!
No fuel needed
Just freakishly strong arms
And obviously a (quite)
Stubborn mind.
That bus driver who tried to ignore me
Despite clearly seeing me in Old Reekie
May have left me with no other choice
Than taking a taxi BUT only
After I chased him downhill
(2 stops)
And back up
(1 stop, get real, give up).
Seattle, San Francisco, Santorini,
I survived them all!
My wheels often didn't
Particularly when flying,

Or wheeling this quadruple marathon,
  Over two months
    Mostly in Scotland
      All in winter...
There were some close calls
Injured wrists
Dislocated and
Broken fingers.
I am not invincible.
Stairs are my downfall
Rain my enemy
(No grip, no brakes)
But when I wheel, I AM free!
In the Great Plain of Hungary
My other home, my city,
I wheel all day
I wheel all night
I drink and drive
(legally!)
There is no greater feeling
No better freedom
Than wheeling home, alone,
In the middle of the night
Headphones on
Music blaring.
Walkers find tho thirty
Minutes journey too
long but I
    Want
      More!
By the time I arrive,
Slot the key in,
Gate ready to open,
I often really, truly
Want to cry.
Not tears of despair
    Of sadness
      Of loss
This is crying out of joy
    Of relief
      Of wonder
At the amazing freedom
My wheels give me,

Of having got my
Life
Back.
I am a wheeler
I most probably always will be.
But that's OK.
This, is ME. ⫽

Devolution of the Species

Ben Jones

I'm tired of living in the air
I think I'd rather be
A counter evolutionist
And crawl into the sea
Develop gills, eject my limbs
Farewell my vertebrae
Reclining with the jelly fish
Beyond the reach of day
I'll clamber down the food chain
Leave humans to their plight
Screw you Mr Darwin
The amoebas had it right ⁄⁄

Westwood

John Fewings

Fuzzy-felt moon
Stitched against a purple sky,
Lacquered black tower
Guarding sleepy pasture.
Cattlemen and traders,
Vagabonds and Flemish sailors,
All have trod these pathways
That wend across the Westwood.
To homes and embered hearths,
To taverns full for market day
Or, wearying their final trek
Along the path beside the Beck
That leads to leather-laden barges
Moored at Grevale haven.

And walking back from Walkington,
Something of their history,
Something of their industry,
Some part of their community
Hugs and close embraces me
As do those Minster towers,
Harbingers of sanctuary
Now lit with electricity
That gleam against a purple sky
And beam a "Welcome home". ⁄⁄

Biographies

Adrienne Silcock
published her first poetry pamphlet *Taking Responsibility for the Moon* (Mudfog) in 2014. Her first novel *Vermin* (Flambard) was published in 2000. *Controlling Aphrodite* was shortlisted for the Virginia Prize 2009. *The Kiss* is published on kindle.

Alan Gillott
is co-host of *The Spoken Word* open mic in York and offers challenging workshops in poetry and performance. Publications include *The Nightcap Book*, Blue Dragon Press, and *Community of Poets* Issue 20, the Connecticut Poetry Society's *Long River Run*, Turn of the River Press' *Wednesdays at Curleys*; the University of Toledo's *Poems for Peace* and he has featured in *Dream Catcher*. Alan is a member of the *Sounds Lyrical Project* of classical composers and poets working together to write new songs; and has featured in England, Europe, and the United States.

Becca Miles
is a twenty-two-year-old former student, currently job seeking and trying to write a novel in her spare time. She has been writing poetry and short stories since she was thirteen. She loves science-fiction and fantasy, and can often be found in elaborate costumes pretending to be a wizard.

Ben Jones
is a life-long poet and writer. He lives in Yorkshire with his long term partner and two children. When he's not annoying the former and avoiding the latter, he is usually found behind

a keyboard, drowning in coffee and giggling through sleep deprivation.

Christopher Nosnibor
is a writing machine. The author of anti-novels *The Plagiarist* and *This Book is Fucking Stupid*, he is currently touring the ever-evolving spoken-word project *The Rage Monologues* to the shock, bewilderment and terror of audiences around England.

Clint Wastling
is a short story writer and performance poet. His first novel, *The Geology of Desire*, was published by Stairwell Books. *Tyrant Rex* – a dystopian Sci-fi novel will also be published by them in late 2017.

Dave Younger
is from Leeds and performs open mic poetry at spoken word events around Yorkshire. He also writes short fiction and political journalism and makes visual art. He's been published in the UK, USA, China and Pakistan.

Glen Taylor
is an ex-York student of English Literature looking to start an MA in Creative Writing in 2017. He writes prose and poetry, and enjoys experimenting with form, but usually takes too long about it.

Grant Tarbard
is a poet based in Essex. His poems have appeared widely in journals such as *The Rialto, London Grip* and *A New Ulster*. His pamphlet *Loneliness is the Machine that Drives the World* (Platypus Press) is out now.

Hannah Stone
London-born Hannah stone has lived in Leeds since 1989. Her poetry articulates human encounters with fellow creatures, the landscape and various pasts. Her first solo collection, *Lodestone*, was published in 2016. She collaborates with other poets and composers.

Harry Gallagher
has been published by The Interpreter's House, Poets' Republic, Rebel Poetry, Lucifer Press, 3 Drops From The Cauldron and many others. His third pamphlet, *Chasing The Sunset (*Black Light Engine Room Press), is available online.

Jacqueline Zacharias
writes about ghosts, river gods, Asian marriages (some with ghosts, some with gods, some just with awful family members) and has a surreal and oftentimes quite humourous take on our modern world. Jacqueline is a vibrant reader and York wishes she could attend more events to share her astonishing work.

Jennie Owens
is a teacher of creative writing and has been widely published in anthologies and magazines including *Envoi, Iota, The Reader and Ink, Sweat and Tears*, and of *course Dream Catcher*!

Joe Williams
is a writer and performing poet from Leeds, and the creator of *Haiku Hole*. He performs regularly at events in Yorkshire and beyond, and is very cheap.

John Fewings
recently retired from a varied teaching career, John lives in the thriving market town of Beverley devoting much of his time to writing. As a member of the *Argy-Bargy Poets*, he has performed at venues across the East Riding of Yorkshire and beyond.

John Gilham
edits *Dream Catcher* literary magazine. As well as poetry, pubs and beer, he likes railways, London, cycling, European Travel and time with his grandchildren. *Fosdyke and Me and Other Poems* (2009), and *Learning to Breathe* (2015) are published by Stairwell Books.

Louise Mason
is a new exhibitionist having rediscovered her passion for poetry last year at the York Spoken Word. She is a black belt in Tae Kwon Do, enjoys walking barefoot on the beach, drinking red wine and listening to Northern Soul.

Mark Connors
is a poet/novelist from Leeds, UK. He's had over 80 poems published in the UK and overseas. Mark's debut poetry pamphlet, *Life is a Long Song* was published by OWF Press in 2015. His first collection will be published in 2017.

Matt L. T. Smith
is a Hampshire performance poet. His work ranges from the

personal to the political, approaching both with fierce fervour. Matt is part of Kane Holborn's organisation *AnyStage,* which tackles accessibility within the arts, where he performs both his own poetry and Kane's.

Muireall
Muriel Masson, also known as Muireall, is a performer, poet, chanteuse and musician from Scotland with added French and Hungarian influences. The wheeling and stick-wielding doc gets her inspiration from her numerous identities and multiple countries. Muireall first performed at a Stairwell Books launch in York in 2014.

Paul Sutherland
is a British-Canadian writer immigrating to the UK 1973. He founded the journal *Dream Catcher* in 1996. He has eleven poetry collections published. Recently *New and Selected Poems* from Valley Press, 2016. He's appeared in anthologies including *The Exhibitionists* and *York* by Stairwell Books.

P J Quinn
Mother and daughter Pauline Kirk and Jo Summers have written three DI Ambrose Mysteries as PJ Quinn (published by Stairwell Books). Pauline is a York poet and novelist. Surrey-based Jo writes for the legal press. A fourth mystery, *Poetic Justice*, is in progress.

Rose Drew
is annoyed by nonsense like inequality, misogyny, and tourists who stop short in the street. Rose, political activist, poet-anthropologist and mom, has co-hosted York Spoken Word for 11yrs, and co-owns Stairwell Books. Her favourite places: a lab analysing skeletons; in front of a large audience, hollering poetry. Rose would love to see her NSA file.

Ross Moore
was born in Birmingham in 1957 and educated at Moseley School of Art in the city. He wanted to paint from the age of seven and although painting remains his first love, wordsmithery has also sat well with me. Currently he is reworking a series of religious themes from a popular book series and painting images from Morocco.

Sue Lister
Her passion for the theatre has taken her to New Zealand and Canada as a drama teacher, actor and director. She doesn't write poetry unless there is a gap in a show that she feels

moved to fill. She now delights in being the Artistic Director of *The Real People Theatre* and having her finger in many pies having "resurged" rather than "retired"!

Tom Dixon
attended his first spoken word event earlier this year and read *Delete* as his debut piece. His second was probably too rude to print. He lives in York with his wife and daughter and is currently working on his debut novel.

Val Horner
is a keen participant at The Spoken Word open mic who lives in York on the banks of The Foss. Her poems may be found in anthologies published by Stairwell Books, *Paragram* (Four Point Press) *Live Canon Ltd.* and *Ware Poets* (Rockingham Press).

Index of Authors

Other anthologies and collections available from Stairwell Books

For further information please contact rose@stairwellbooks.com

www.stairwellbooks.co.uk
@stairwellbooks